HELLER

25 MELODIOUS STUDIES

OPUS 45 FOR THE PIANO

EDITED BY WILLARD A. PALMER

CONTENTS

FOREWORD

Stephen Heller was born in Budapest in 1813 and died in Paris in 1888. He enjoyed great success, both as a concert pianist and as a composer. He was admired and encouraged by Chopin, Schumann and Liszt, who were his close friends.

Heller's Opus 16, entitled *The Art of Phrasing*, consisted of 24 etudes. It was such a success that it guaranteed his economic security and enabled him to devote most of his time to composing. He had even greater success with the present work, *25 Melodious Studies,* Opus 45, which was written at the urging of his publisher as an introduction to his Opus 16.

The selections contained in Opus 45 are worthy of comparison with the shorter piano pieces of Schumann, such as those found in *The Album for the Young,* and with some of Mendelssohn's *Songs Without Words.* Heller's music shows the influence of both of these composers, but is nevertheless quite original.

The titles of the pieces in Opus 45 are very probably not Heller's own, and may have been added by the publisher. Heller is known to have said that descriptive titles were not important, since "music should be evocative rather than descriptive." At any rate, some of the titles, such as "A Real Task" and "Sterness," do little to add to the attractiveness of these pieces for modern-day students, and are best changed or omitted. We have retitled the former of these two "A Challenge," and the latter, "Scherzo."

This new edition corrects a number of printing errors and omissions. It is openly spaced for easier reading, but is without poor page-turns. Editorial suggestions appear in footnotes, and each piece is introduced with a short description of the style and/or purpose of the selection.

WILLARD A. PALMER

Second Edition
Copyright © MMI by Alfred Publishing Co., Inc.
Cover art: Golden Autumn
by Isaac Levitan
Tretyakov Gallery, Moscow, Russia
Scala/Art Resource, NY

In this quiet piece the right-hand sixteenth notes should be legato and equal throughout. The left-hand phrasing should be carefully observed, but not exaggerated.

THE BROOK

In contrast to the quiet and evenly flowing brook depicted in the previous work in this book, the avalanche portrayed in this piece is surging and rolling with unpredictable changes in dynamics, touch and phrasing. Accents should be strongly emphasized, *fortes* quite loud, and *piano* indications meticulously observed.

THE AVALANCHE

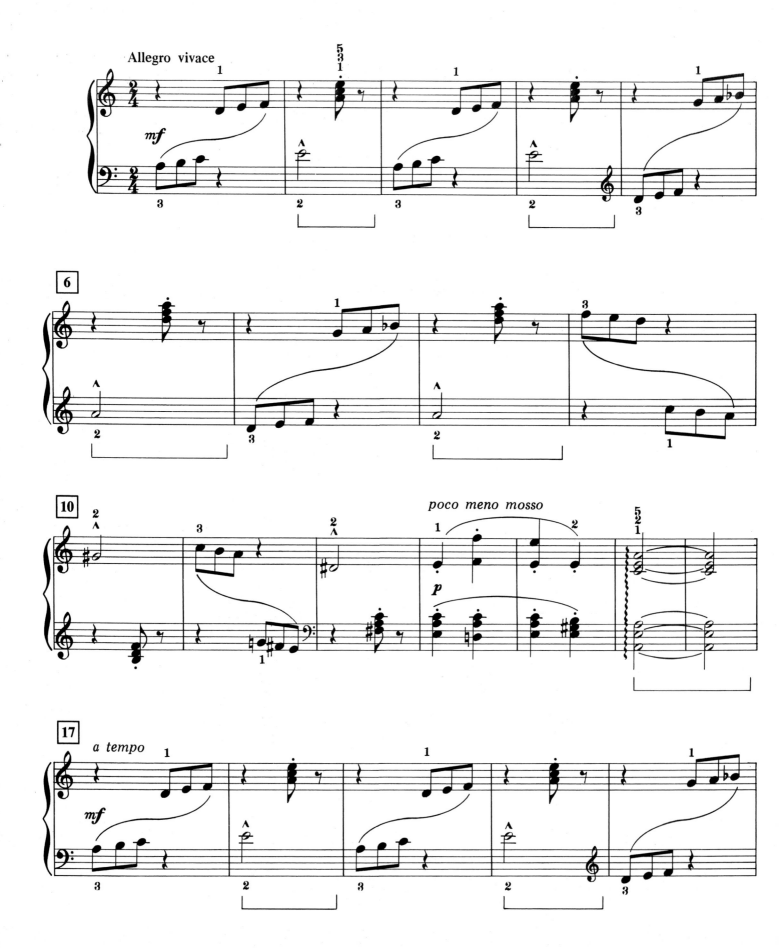

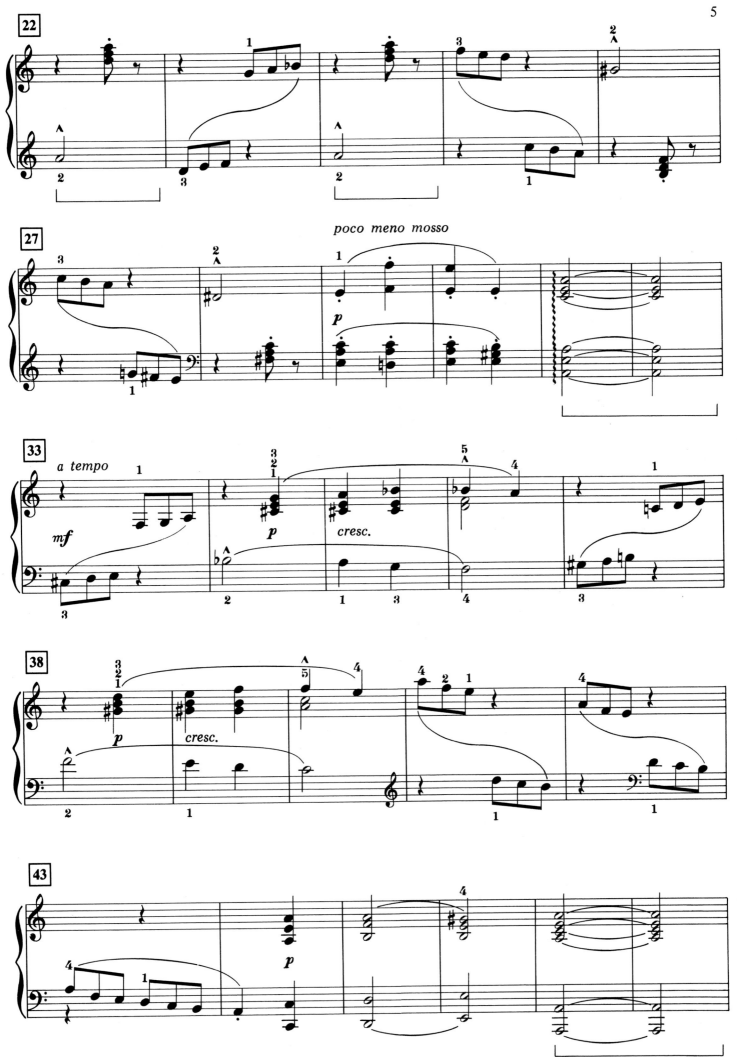

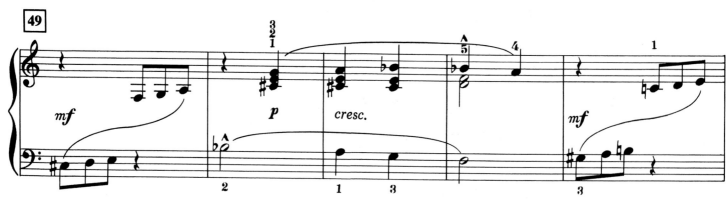

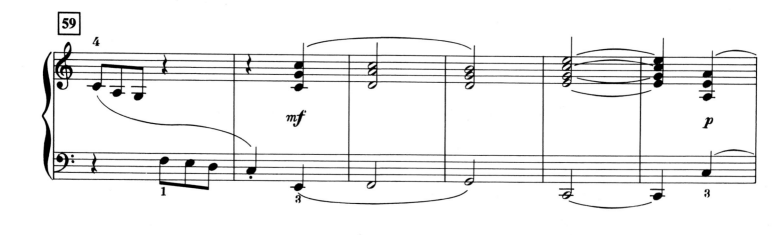

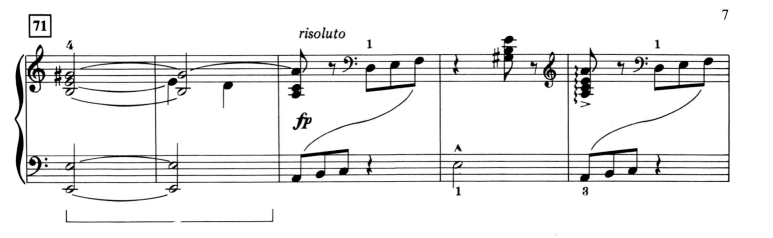

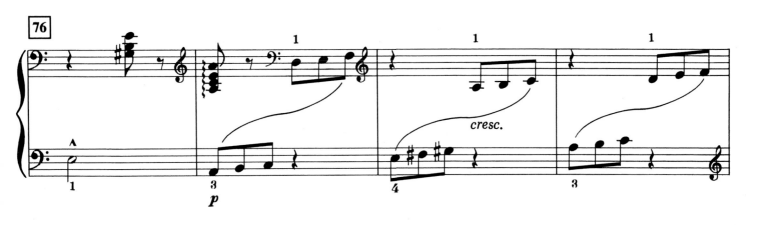

8

This interesting work, with broken chord figures in the right hand against scale passages in the left hand, lives up to its name. Students who master it will make technical progress, and will improve coordination between the hands as well as finger independence. They will also have learned a brilliant and effective piano solo for recital performance.

A CHALLENGE

This piece is a study in contrasting moods. Flowing legato sections are interrupted by forceful chordal passages which employ staccato and tenuto chords. Careful observance of indications for touch, phrasing and dynamics is necessary for maximum effectiveness.

SORROW AND JOY

12

This is a "song without words" in the truest sense, in the tradition of Felix Mendelssohn. The Italian word *comodo* in the opening tempo indication means "comfortable, convenient, moderate." This means the tempo should be a bit restrained, so that it is not forced in the least. The selection should be played in a *cantabile* or "singing" style. The phrasing indications must be carefully observed.

SONG OF MAY

13

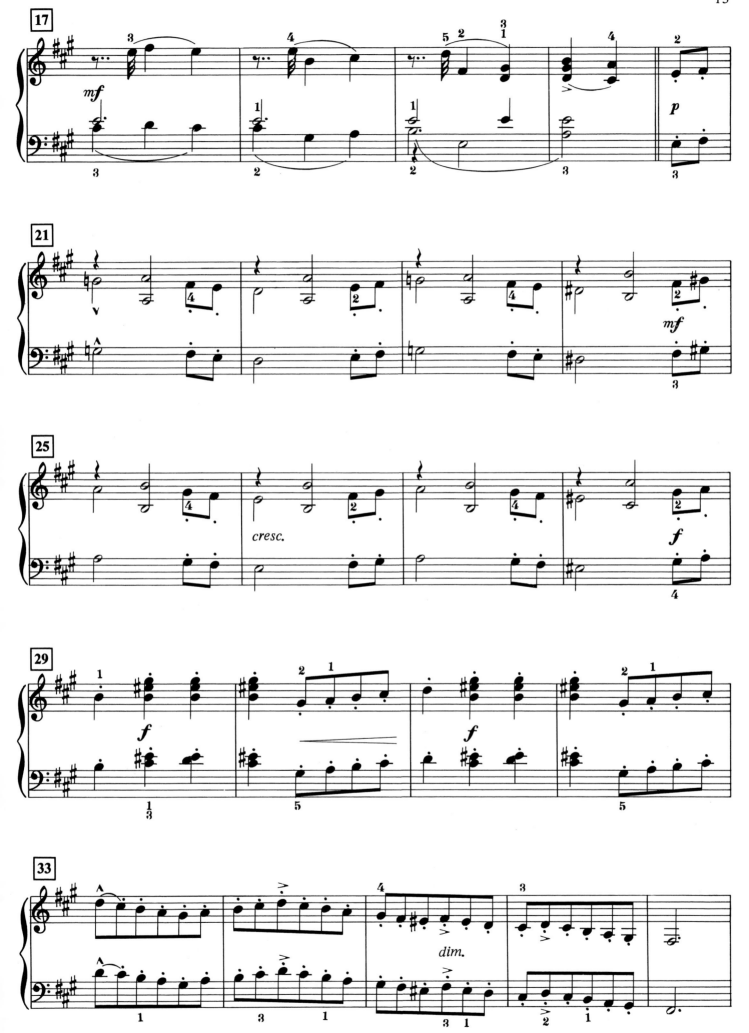

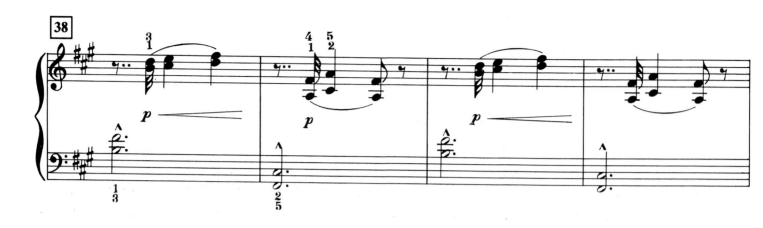

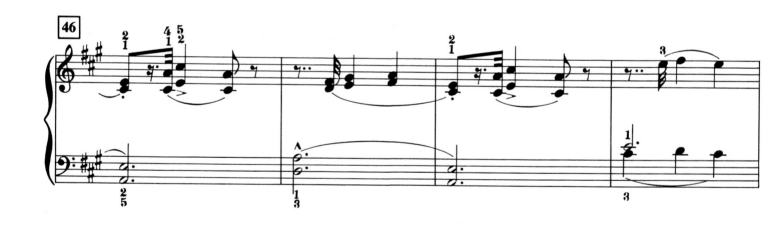

DANSE TRISTE means "Sad Dance." It is possible that Heller gave the tempo as *allegro con moto* to avoid a dragging tempo. It should sound quite relaxed, and certainly should be played no faster than ♩ = 108.

DANSE TRISTE

a Perdendosi : dying away

(b) Play the small notes as *short appoggiaturas,* very quickly, almost simultaneously with the following large note.

To get the proper effect from this piece, play the staccato notes in the left hand so they sound like the *pizzicato* produced by plucking the strings of a bass violin.

DETERMINATION

(a) Play the small note very quickly, on the beat.

20

A BARCAROLLE is more than a simple "Boat Song." It is generally associated with the songs of the Venetian gondoliers. In this one the "singer" seems to be a *basso,* since the principal melody is in the left hand. This lower voice should be prominent at all times. The right hand does contain some important and very effective countermelodies. Careful observance of the *crescendos* and *diminuendos* indicated by the composer will bring all the voices into proper relief.

BARCAROLLE

In this modern day, the title might be taken to mean "Music of the Spheres." The melody, played with the right-hand thumb, should be clearly heard at all times.

CELESTIAL VOICES

ⓐ Play the small note quickly, almost simultaneously with the following large note. Be sure to catch the small note with the pedal, since it becomes the bass note in this measure. The same is true in measure 28.

In this selection, the longer notes form a hymnlike chorale, against which the eighth-note triplets must be played softly by comparison, since they function as an accompaniment.

VESPER SONG

This is a study in rapidly repeated pairs of notes. They should be fingered 3, 2 as Heller indicates. At a slow tempo the repetition of the same finger may seem easier, but it is very difficult to attain the required speed with a totally relaxed hand, unless the fingers are changed on the repeated notes. Begin slowly and gradually work up to *allegro*.

SLEETING

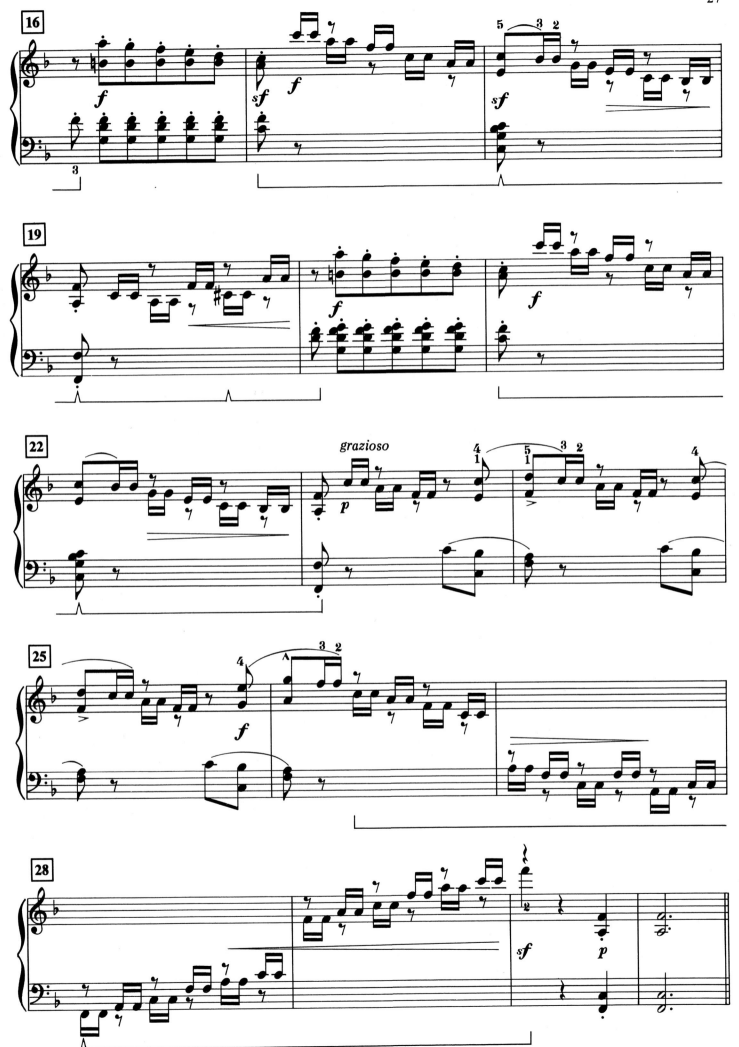

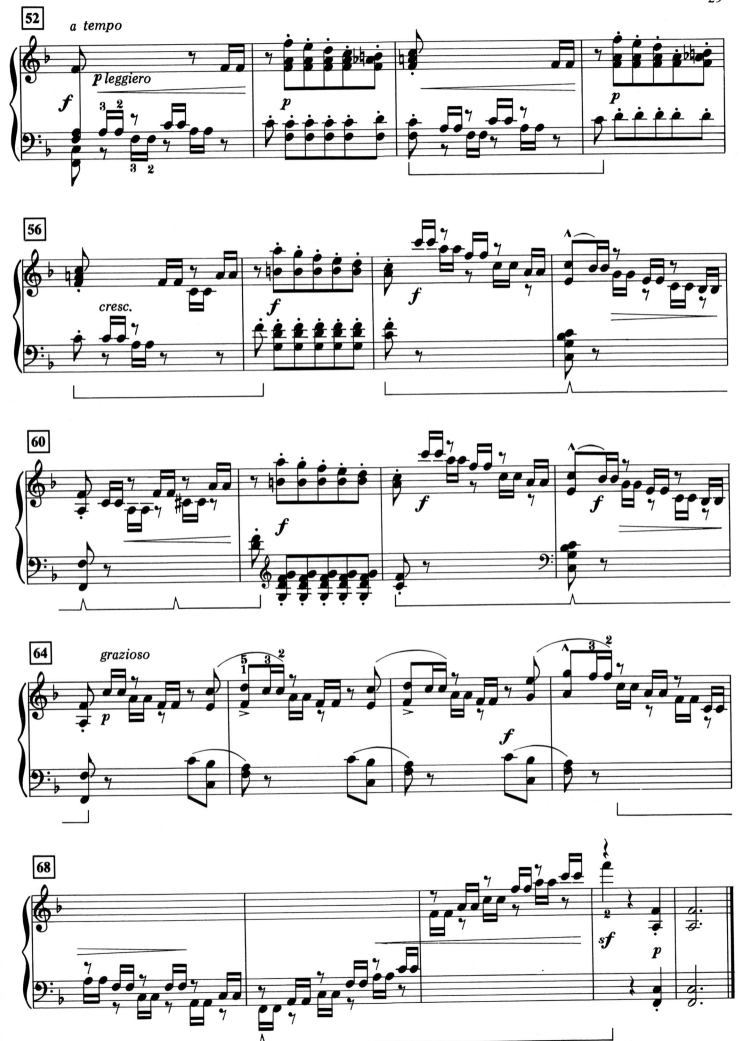

Although some compilers have titled this piece STERNNESS, its rollicking, almost mischievous character is reminiscent of some of Mendelssohn's puckish music from A MIDSUMMER NIGHT'S DREAM. The *staccato* indications in the last five measures must be carefully observed, and there should be not a trace of *ritardando* at the end.

SCHERZO

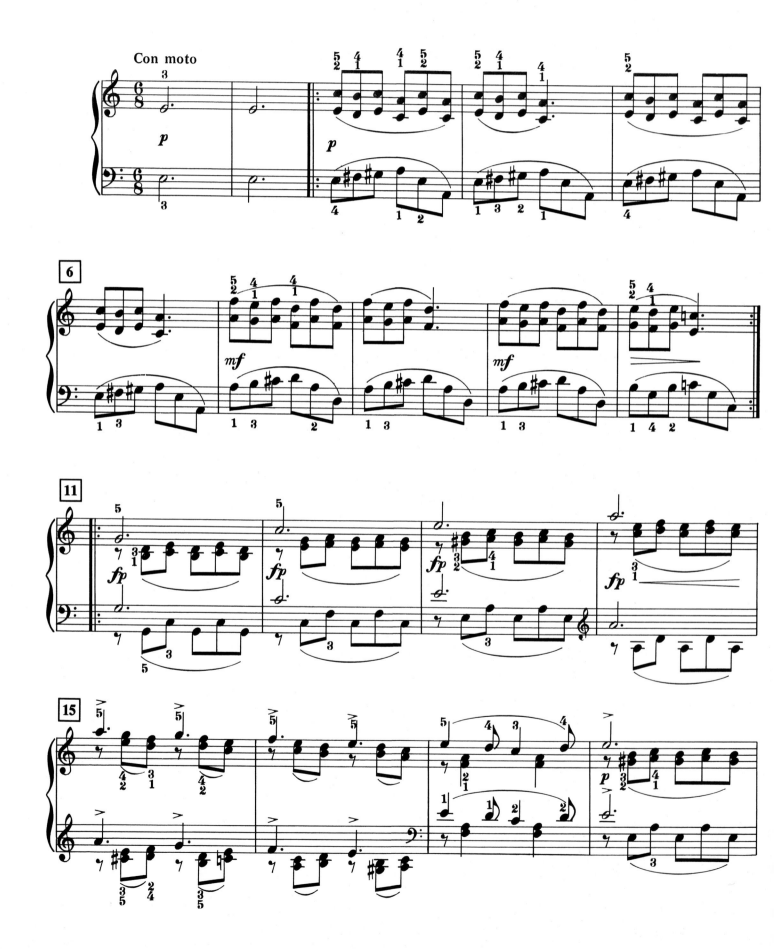

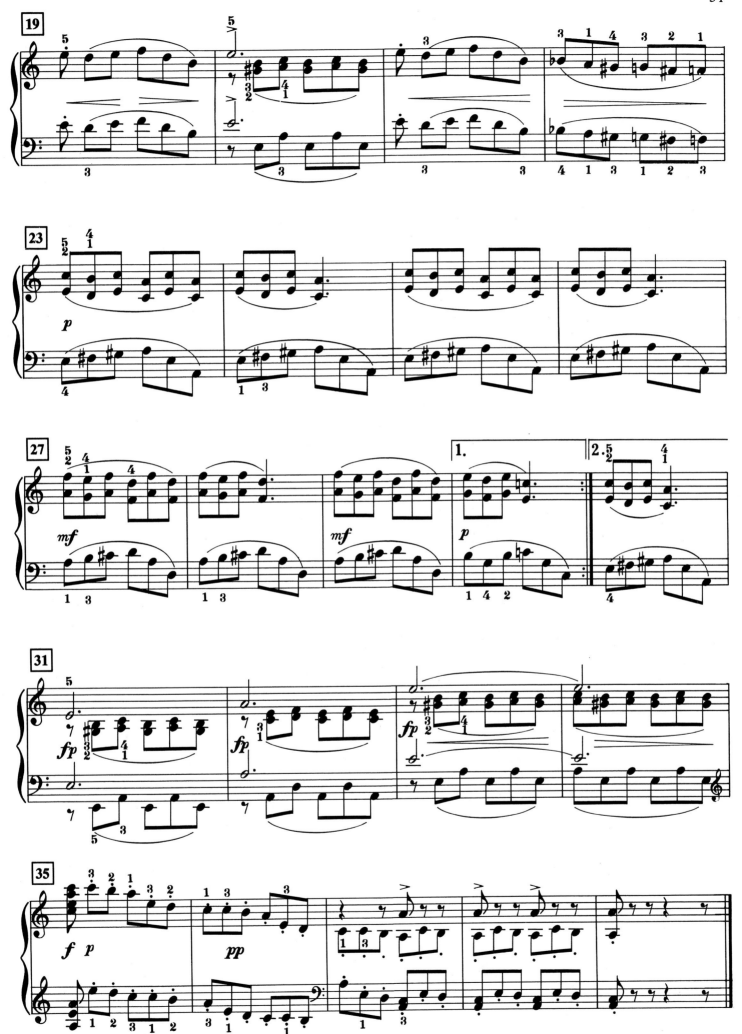

This selection, with its long skips in the left-hand part, and its scale and arpeggio passages in the right hand, is a great technic-builder as well as an effective and popular solo piece. It should be played with great lightness, with both hands completely relaxed throughout.

WALTZ

ⓐ Play the small notes as short appoggiaturas, very quickly, almost simultaneously with the following large note.

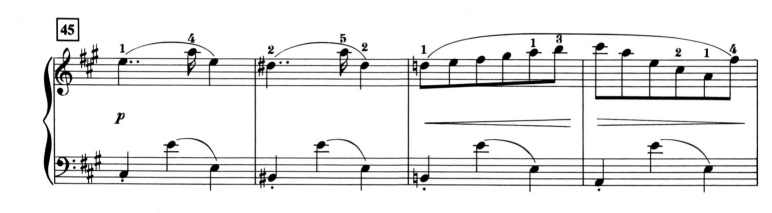

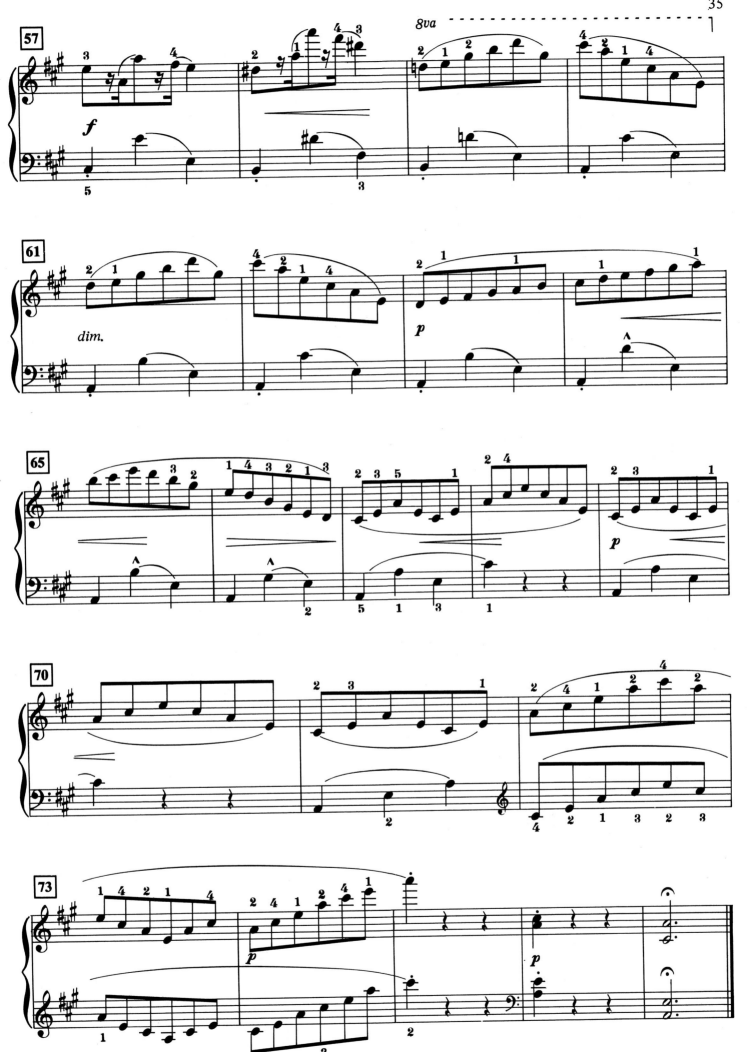

This selection, a "song without words" in the Mendelssohn tradition, is one of Heller's most popular pieces. Play the repeated notes with a light and relaxed "wrist-staccato." Let the left-hand melody sing out prominently in measures 1 – 8 and 28 – 35. Carefully observe pedal indications and dynamics.

SAILOR'S SONG

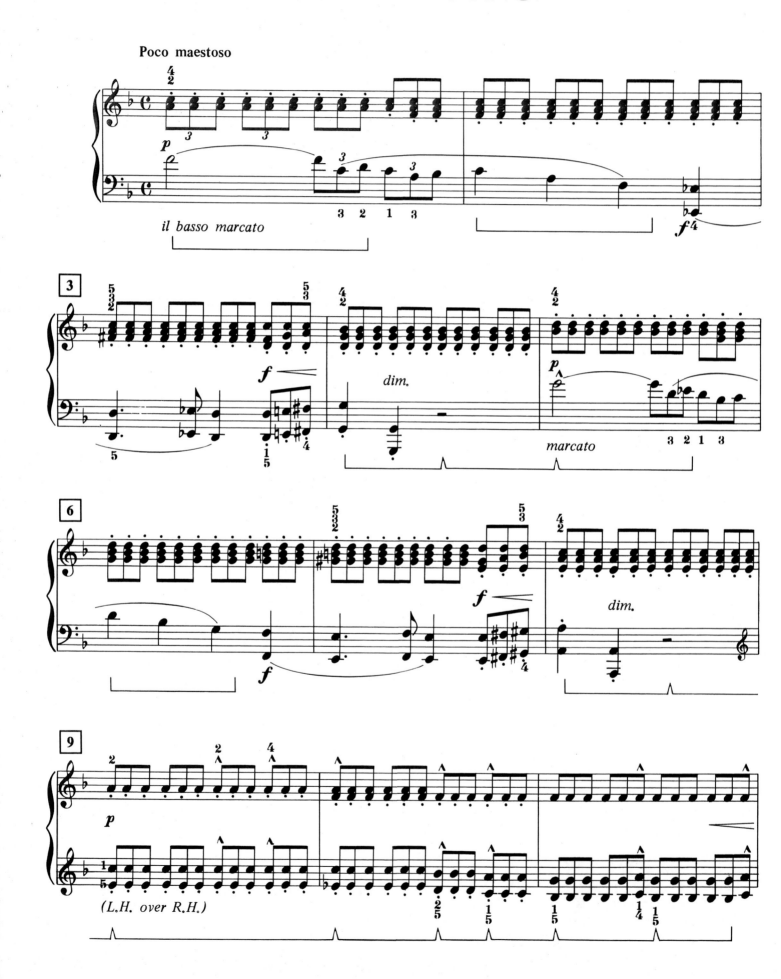

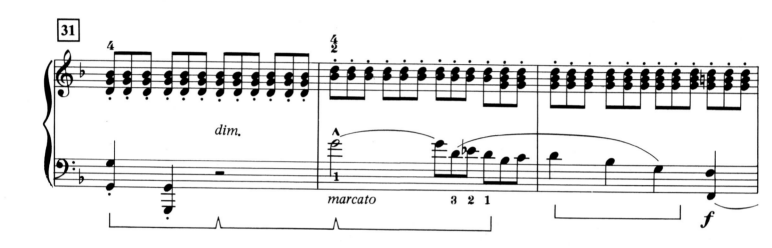

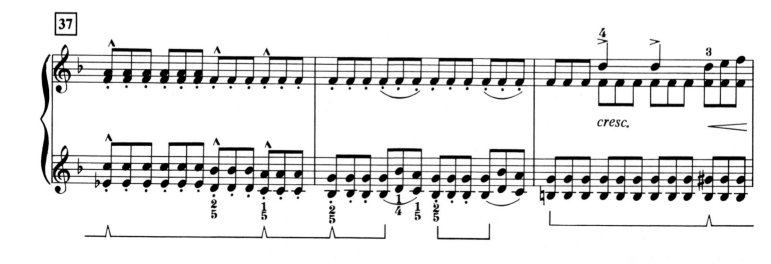

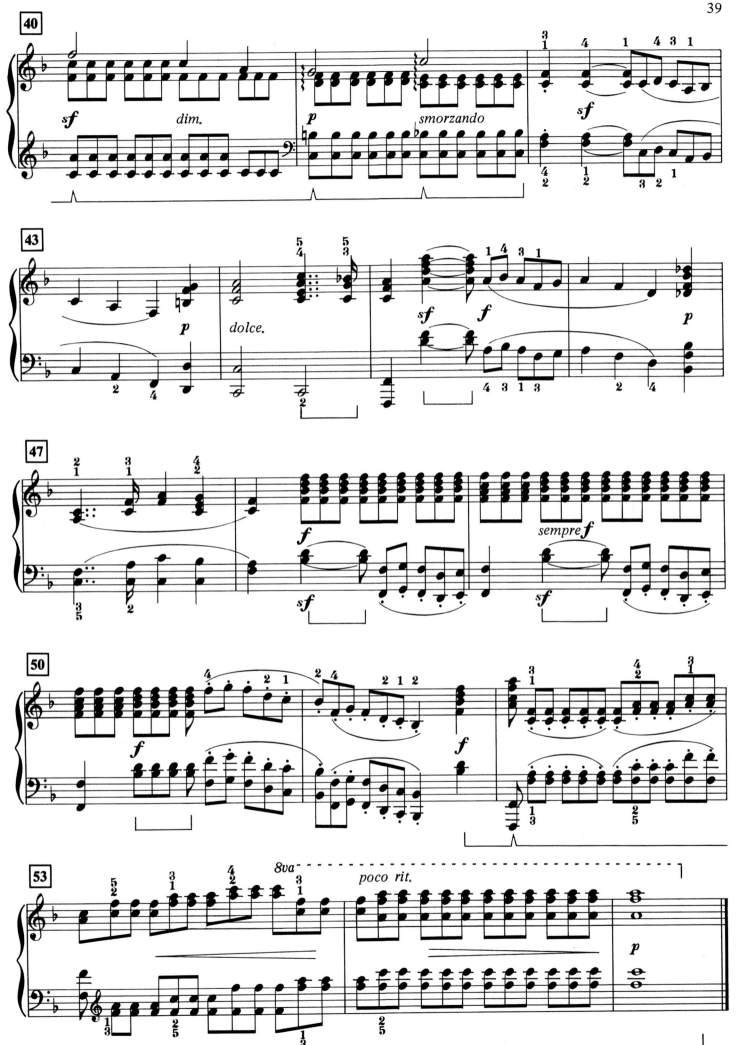

This powerful selection is another "song without words." The massive chords must be brought out with considerable weight of arms and body. Carefully observe the sudden piano chords which occur, echolike, in several places.

WARRIOR'S SONG

In Heller's day, IL PENSEROSO, meaning "The Pensive One," was a very popular title for meditative musical selections, particularly piano solos. The title is taken from one of the greatest works of the English poet, John Milton. This piece, like the two previous ones, is a "song without words." The melody in the left hand must be played in a singing style, and must always be clearly heard above the accompanying notes of the right hand.

IL PENSEROSO

ⓐ Play the small note very quickly, almost simultaneously with the following large note.

46

The title NOVELETTE was introduced into music by Schumann, who said "this title is to be taken as the equivalent of a 'romantic story'." This selection, the most ambitious one in Heller's Op. 45 up to this point, is a light and tuneful piece with a contrasting middle section. It will be easier to master if it is practiced quite slowly before being brought up to the indicated *allegro vivace* tempo.

NOVELETTE

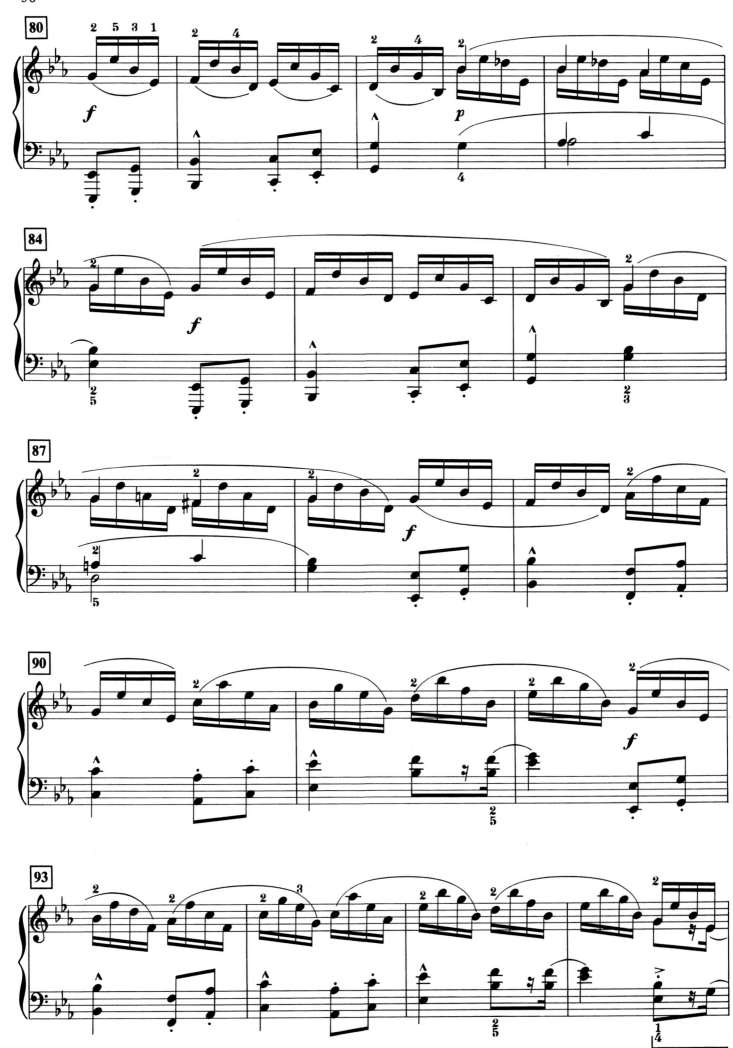

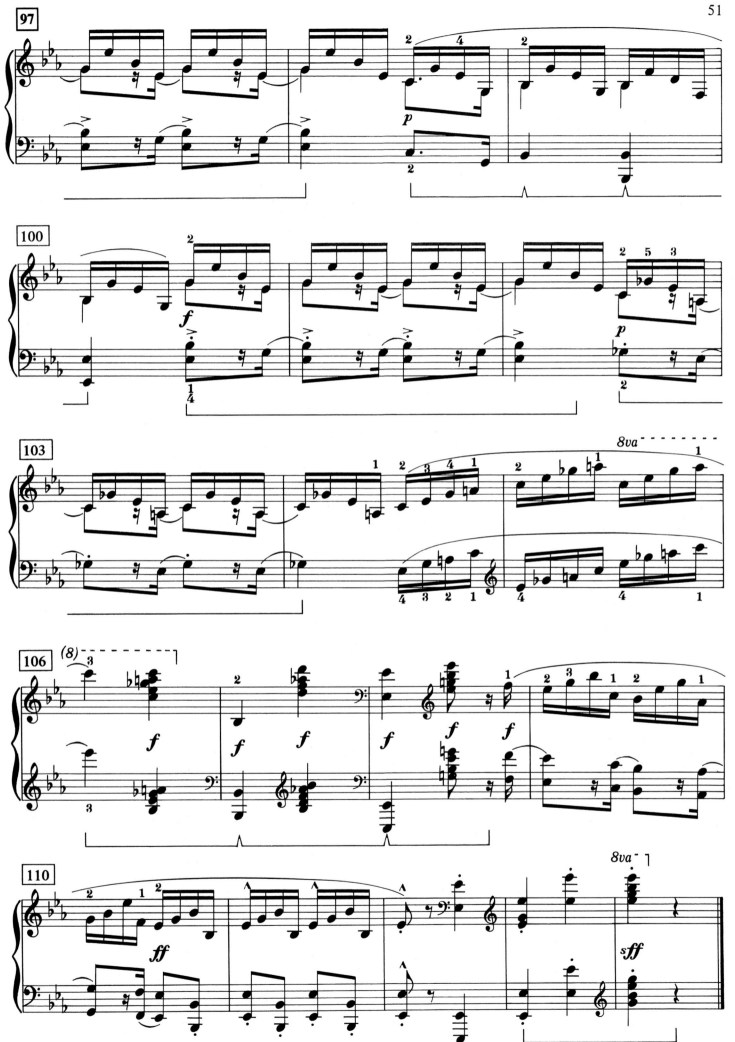

This turbulent piece is a technic-builder. Its restless effect is heightened when the sudden accents, the *crescendos* and *diminuendos* and other dynamic indications, are carefully observed.

IMPATIENCE

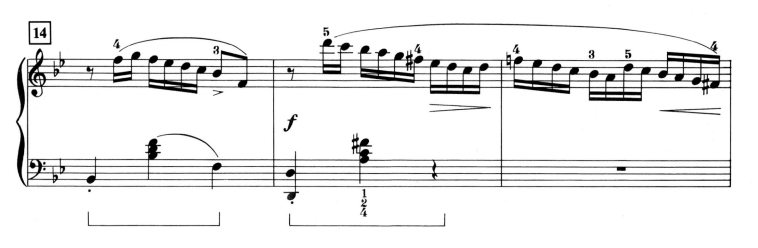

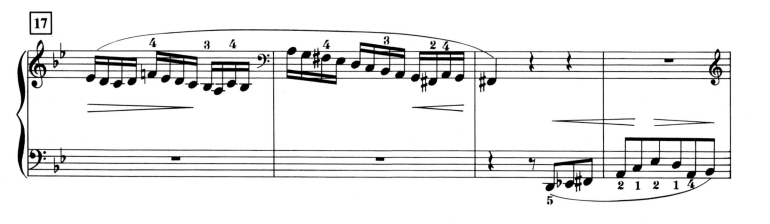

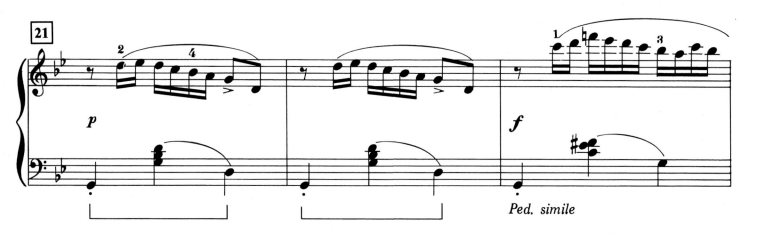

This is an ingenious "trill-study," in which both the right hand and left hand are required to play trill-like figures and other notes simultaneously. The effect, when it is mastered, is that of a technical *tour de force*. Slow practice will be rewarded. The selection is an effective and brilliant solo piece.

SPINNING SONG

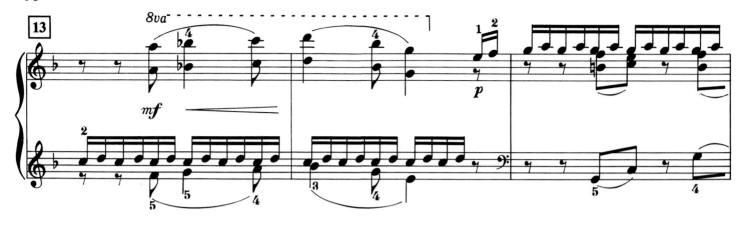

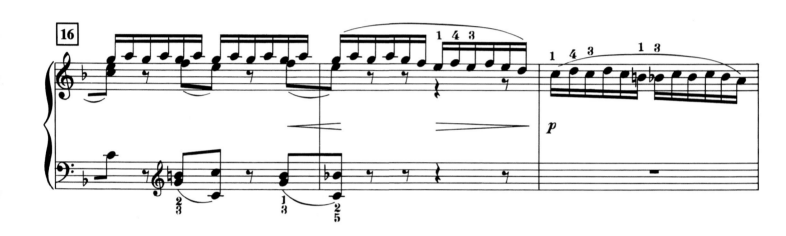

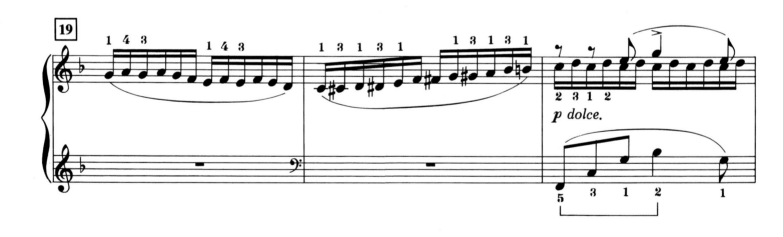

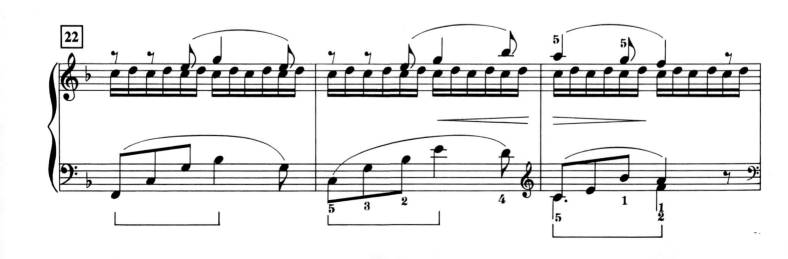

The light, staccato left-hand accompaniment must be kept under the right-hand melody at all times. Dynamics should be carefully observed throughout. The tempo must be kept absolutely even and steady, except in the *ritenuto* in measures 44 and 45.

THE BALLET

(a) Play the small note as a short appoggiatura, very quickly, almost simultaneously with the following large note.

62

This is an excellent study for the development of technic. There are many subtle effects of dynamics and also of touch, such as the use of legato arpeggios in the left hand against staccato notes in the right hand. The entire piece should be played with a relaxed, light and airy style in keeping with the imaginative title. Practice slowly before playing up to tempo.

SPRITES AND MERMAIDS

(a) Small notes should be played very quickly, on the beat.

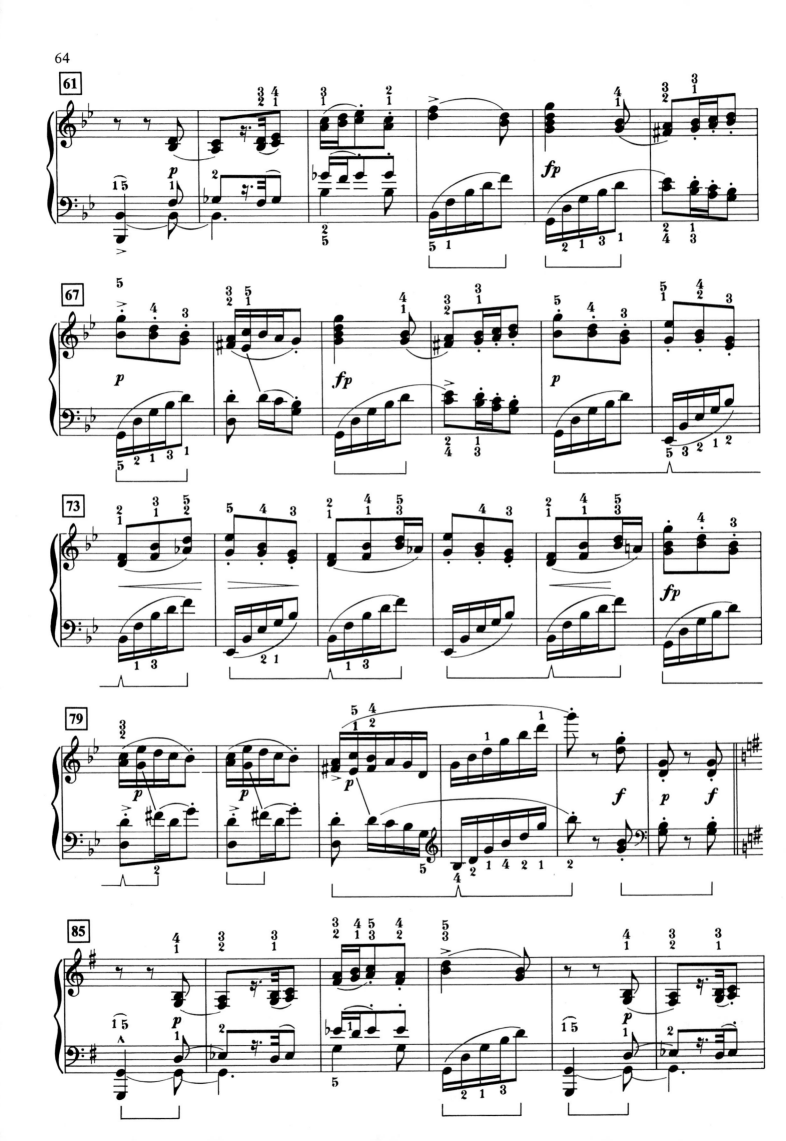

This study in arpeggiation features a melody played with alternating left and right hand, beginning with the last treble note of measure 9. This melody must always be brought out above the accompanying arpeggio figures.

SONG OF THE HARP

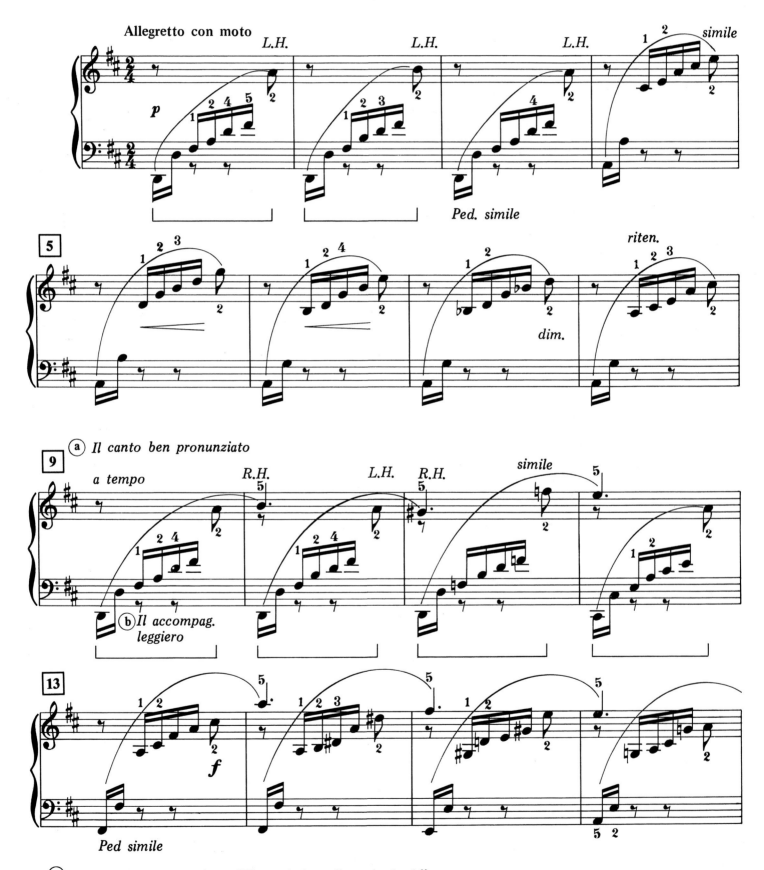

(a) Il canto ben pronunziato: "The melody well emphasized."
(b) Il accompag. leggiero: "The accompaniment lightly played."

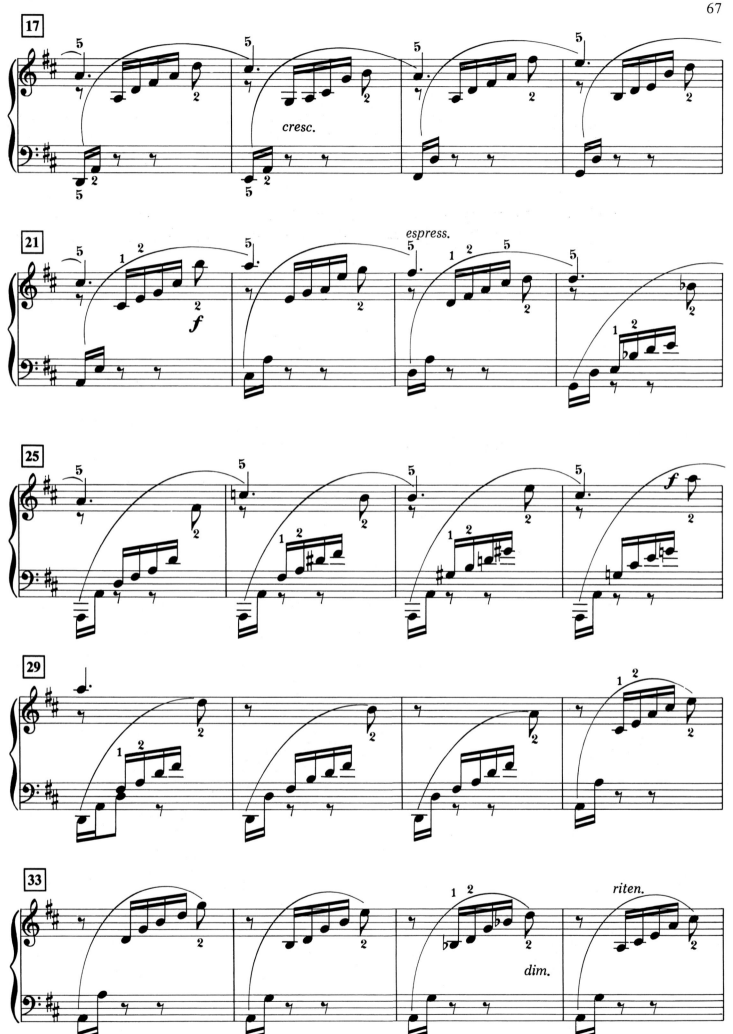

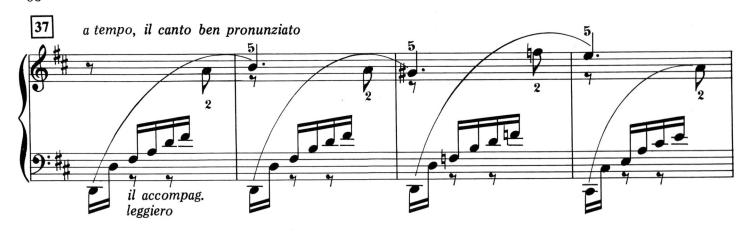

a tempo, il canto ben pronunziato

il accompag.
leggiero

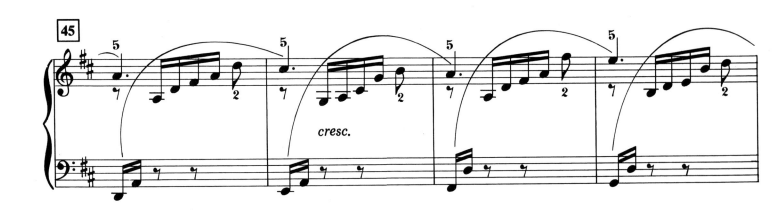

cresc.

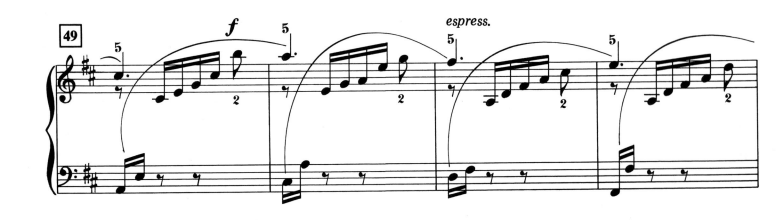

espress.

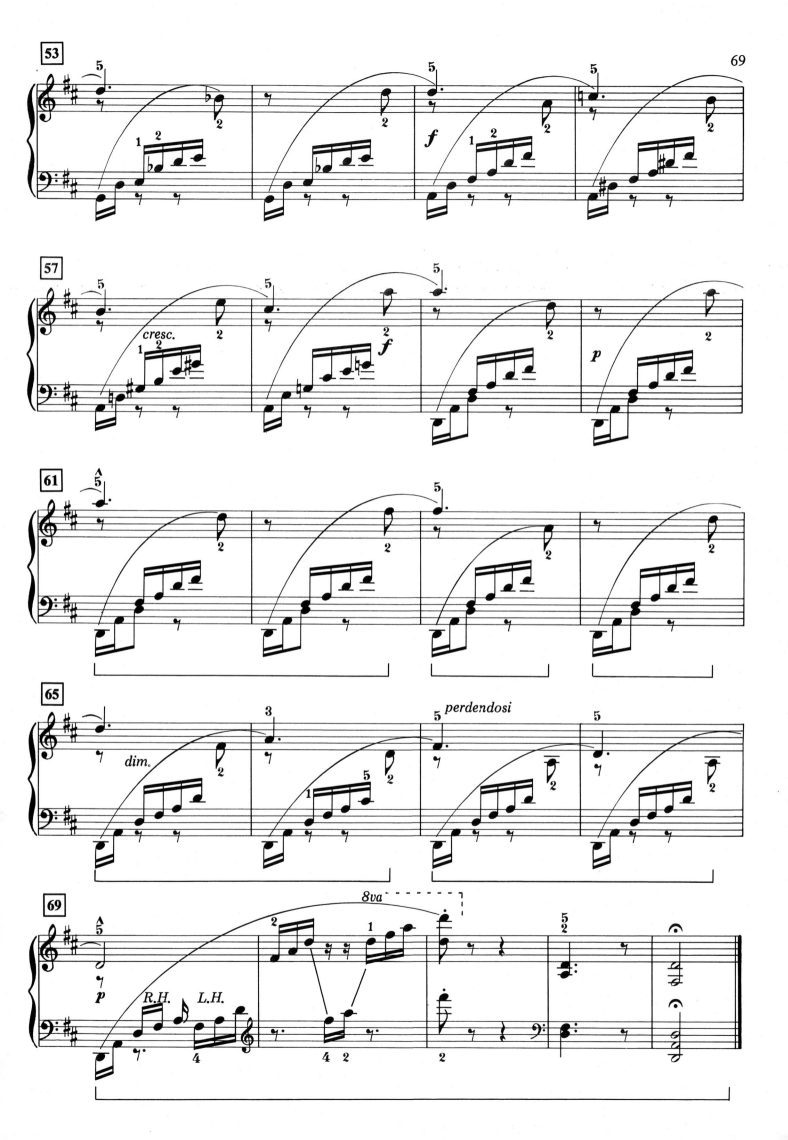

This is a spectacular selection, an excellent technic-builder for left hand. Much of its effectiveness depends, however, on the careful observance of the accents, touch and phrasing of the right-hand notes.

THROUGH WIND AND RAIN

The broken chords in the right-hand part of this selection should have a continuous "rolling" effect. The breaks between slurs should be practically imperceptible, since they were intended to convey a continuous legato with a very slight emphasis on the first note of each slur. Play the left-hand staccato notes very crisply, with light wrist action.

OVER HILL AND DALE

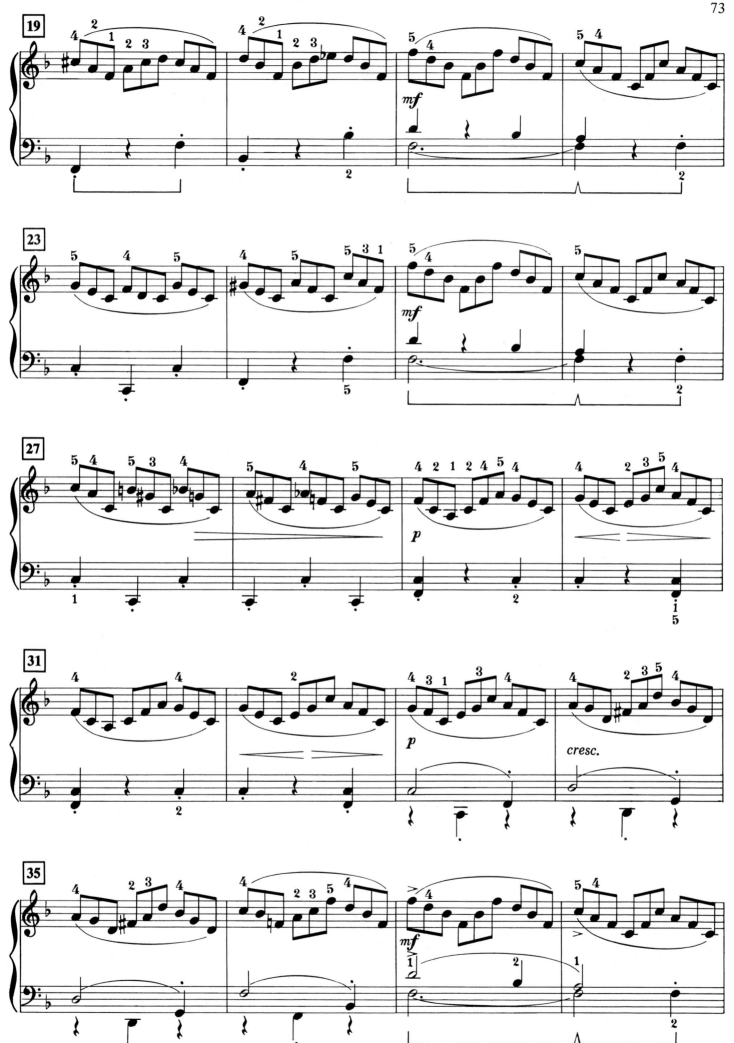

This effective showpiece with which Heller concludes his Opus 45 requires a very relaxed wrist to achieve the almost continuous staccato of the opening sections. The contrasting legato of the *allegretto* section, beginning with measure 82, is taken from The Brook, the first piece in Opus 45, and is brought into relief through the use of overlapping pedal. The selection concludes bombastically, with massive chords against *tremolando* bass.

EPILOGUE

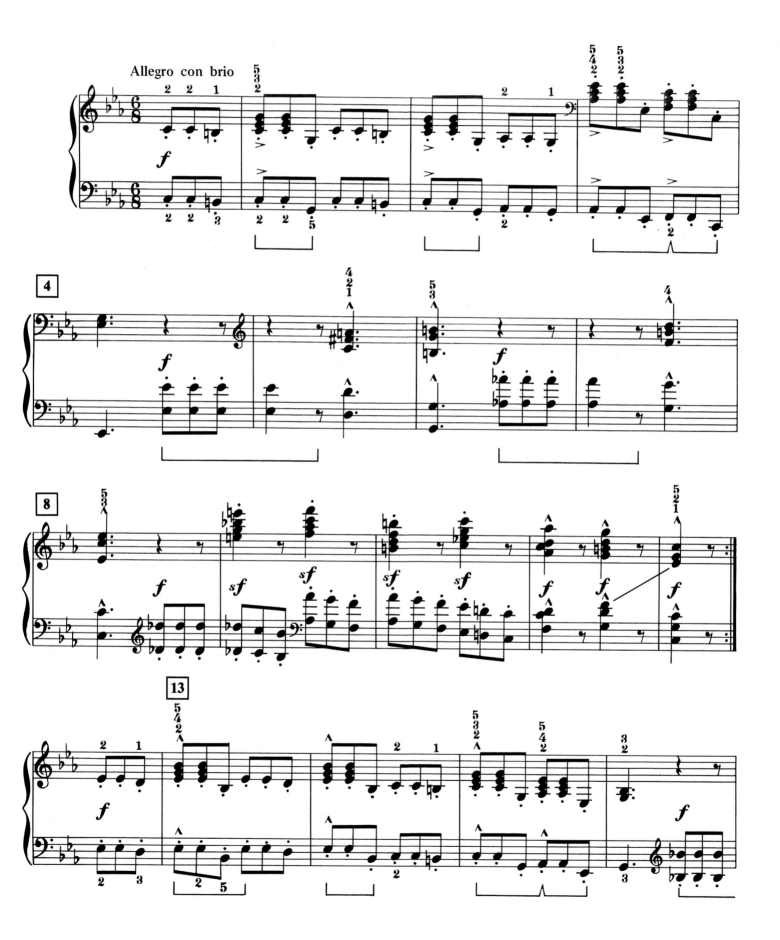